A STUDY IN KARMA

Owing to the antiquity and rarity of this book, certain pages are regrettably absent, and readability is compromised due to the blurring of the original text. If you possess any insights regarding the availability of these missing sections, kindly inform us. Your assistance is crucial in ensuring the completion of this significant work for the benefit of future generations.

A STUDY IN KARMA

ANNIE BESANT

GYAN

Published by

GYAN

Gyan Publishing House
5, Ansari Road
Daryaganj, New Delhi-110002
Phone: 011-47034999, 9811692060
E-mail: books@gyanbooks.com

Distribution Network
gyanbooks.com
India, USA, Canada, UK, Australia

ISBN: 978-93-6780-566-4 (HB)
First Published, 1912

2nd Impression 2024

Printed at: Gyan Press, Delhi.

A STUDY IN KARMA
Author: ANNIE BESANT

A STUDY IN KARMA

A STUDY IN KARMA

BY

ANNIE BESANT

THE THEOSOPHICAL PUBLISHING HOUSE

ADYAR, MADRAS, INDIA

1952

CONTENTS

KARMA

(From *The Light of Asia* by SIR EDWIN ARNOLD)

It knows not wrath nor pardon; utter true
Its measures mete, its faultless balance weighs;
Times are as nought, to-morrow it will judge,
Or after many days.

By this the slayer's knife did stab himself;
The unjust judge hath lost his own defender;
The false tongue dooms its lie; the creeping thief
And spoiler rob, to render.

Such is the Law which moves to righteousness,
Which none at last can turn aside or stay;
The heart of it is Love, the end of it
Is Peace and Consummation sweet. Obey!

A STUDY IN KARMA

AMONG the many illuminating gifts to the western world, conveyed to it by the medium of the Theosophical Society, that of the knowledge of karma comes perhaps next in importance to that of reincarnation. It removes human thought and desire from the region of arbitrary happenings to the realm of law, and thus places man's future under his own control in proportion to the amount of his knowledge.

The main conception of karma, "As a man soweth, so shall he also reap," is easy to grasp. But the application of this to daily life in detail, the method of its working and its far-reaching consequences—these are the difficulties which become more bewildering to the student as his knowledge increases. The principles on which any natural science is based are, for the most part, readily intelligible to people of fair intelligence and ordinary education ; but as the student passes from principles to practice, from outline to details, he discovers that difficulties press upon him, and if he would wholly master his subject he finds himself compelled to become a specialist, and to devote long periods to the unravelling of the tangles which confront him. So is it also with this science of karma; the student cannot remain always in the domain of generalities; he must study the subdivisions of the primary law, must seek to apply it in all the circumstances of life, must learn how far it binds and how freedom becomes possible. He must learn to see in karma a universal law of nature, and learn also, as in face of nature as a whole, that conquest of and rule over her can only be gained by obedience.[1]

Fundamental Principles

In order to understand karma, the student must begin with a clear view of certain fundamental principles, from the lack of which many remain constantly bewildered, asking endless questions which cannot find full solution without the solid laying of this basis. Therefore, in this study, I begin with these, though many of my readers will be already familiar with them, through previous statements of others and myself.

The fundamental conception, on which all later right thinking on karma rests, is that it is law—law, eternal, changeless, invariable, inviolable; law which

[1] "Nature is conquered by obedience."

can never be broken, existing in the nature of things. It is the want of this conception which makes the uninformed Theosophist say: "You must not interfere with his karma." But whenever a natural law is working, you may interfere with it just so far as you can. You do not hear a person say solemnly: "You must not interfere with the law of gravitation." It is understood that gravitation is one of the conditions with which one has to reckon, and that one is perfectly at liberty to counteract any inconvenience it may cause by setting another force against it, by building a buttress to support that which otherwise would fall to the ground under the action of gravitation, or in any other way.

When a condition in nature incommodes us, we use our intelligence to circumvent it, and no one ever dreams of telling us that we must not "interfere with" or change any condition which we dislike. We can only interfere when we have knowledge, for we cannot annihilate any natural force, nor prevent it from acting. But we can neutralize, we can turn aside, its action if we have at command another sufficient force, and while it will never abate for us one jot of its activity, it can be held up, opposed, circumvented, exactly according to our knowledge of its nature and working, and the forces at our disposal. Karma is no more "sacred" than any other natural law; all laws of nature are expressions of the divine nature, and we live and move within them; but they are not mandatory; they are forces which set up conditions amid which we live, and which work in us as well as outside of us; we can manipulate them as we understand them, and as our intelligence unfolds we become more and more their masters, until the man becomes superman, and material nature becomes his servant.

Laws: Natural and Man-made

Much confusion has arisen in this matter because, in the West, "natural" laws have been regarded as apart from mental and moral laws, whereas mental and moral laws are as much part of natural law as the laws of electricity, and all laws are part of the order of nature. Natural law has been, in many minds, confused with human law, and the arbitrariness of human legislation has been imported into the realm of natural law. Laws affecting physical phenomena have been rescued from this arbitrariness by science, but the mental and moral worlds are still in the chaos of lawlessness. Not a divine command, but the immanence of the divine nature conditions our existence, and where prophets have laid down moral laws, these have been declarations of inevitable sequences in the moral world, known to the prophet, unknown to his ignorant hearers; because of their ignorance, his hearers have regarded his declarations as arbitrary commands of a divine lawgiver, sent through him, instead of as mere statements of fact concerning the succession of moral phenomena in a region as orderly as the physical.

Law, in the secondary social sense, is an enactment laid down by an authority regarded as legitimate. It may be the edict of an autocrat, or the act of a legislative assembly; in either case the force of the law depends on the recognition of the authority which makes it. Among the Hindus we find the ideas both of man-made and natural law. The King, in the conception of the Manu, is an autocrat, and the subject must obey; but above the King is a Law to which he in his turn must be obedient, a Law which acts automatically and is in the nature of things. In spite of his autocracy, he is bound by the supreme Law, which will crush him if he disregards it. Weakness oppressed is said to be the most fatal enemy of kings; the tears of the weak sap the foundation of thrones, and the suffering of the nation destroys the ruler. The physical and the superphysical worlds interpenetrate each other, and causes set going in the one bring about results in the other. The King and his Council in ancient India made the laws of the

State, but these were artificial, not natural laws; they were binding on the subjects, and were enforced by penalties, but such laws differ wholly from natural law. It seems a pity that one word should be used for two things so different as natural and artificial laws, yet they are clearly distinguishable by their characteristics.

Artificial laws are changeable; those who make them can alter them or repeal them. Natural laws are unchanging; they cannot be altered nor repealed, but lie in the nature of things. Artificial laws are local, while natural are universal. The law in any country against robbery may be enforced by any penalty chosen by the legislator; sometimes the hand is cut off, sometimes the thief is sent to gaol, sometimes he is hanged. Moreover, the infliction of the penalty is dependent on the discovery of the crime. A penalty which is variable and artificial, and which may be escaped, is obviously not causally related to the crime it punishes. A natural law has no penalty, but one condition follows invariably on another; if a man steals, his nature becomes more thievish, the tendency to dishonesty is increased, and the difficulty of being honest becomes greater; this consequence works in every case, in all countries, and the knowledge or ignorance of others as to the theft makes no difference in the consequence. A penalty which is local, variable and escapable is a sign that the law is artificial, and not natural.

A natural law is a sequence of conditions; such a condition being present, such another condition will invariably follow. If you want to bring about condition No. 2, you must find or make condition No. 1, and then condition No. 2 will follow as an invariable consequence. These sequences never vary when left to themselves, but if a new condition is introduced the succeeding condition will be altered. Thus water runs down a slanting channel in accordance with the force of gravitation, and if you pour water in at the top, it will invariably run down the slope; but you can obstruct the flow by putting an obstacle in the way, and then the resistance which the obstacle opposes to the force of gravitation balances it, but the force of gravitation remains active and is found in the pressure on the obstacle. The first condition is called the cause, the resulting condition the effect, and the same cause always brings about the same effect, provided no other cause is introduced; in the latter case, the effect is the resultant of both.

The Law of Laws

Karma is natural law in the full sense of the term; it is Universal Causation, the Law of Cause and Effect. It may be said to underlie all special laws, all causes and effects. It is natural law in all its aspects and in all its subdivisions; it is not a special law, but a universal condition, the one law whereon all other laws depend, of which all other laws are partial expressions. The *Bhagavad Gīta* says that none who are embodied can escape it—Shining Ones, human beings, animals, vegetables, minerals, are all evolving within this universal law; even the LOGOS Himself, embodied in a universe, comes within a larger sweep of this law of all manifestation. So long as any one is related to matter, embodied in matter, so long is he within karmic law. A being may escape from or transcend one or other of its aspects, but he cannot, while remaining in manifestation, go outside this law.

THE ETERNAL NOW

This universal Law of Causation binds together into one all that happens within a manifestation, for it is universal inter-relation. Inter-relation between all that exists—that is karma. It is therefore coexistent, simultaneous with the coming into existence of any special universe. Therefore karma is eternal as the Universal Self. The inter-relation of everything always is. It never begins; it never ceases to be. "The unreal has no being; the real never ceases to be." Nothing exists isolated, alone, out of relation, and karma is the inter-relation of all that exists. It is manifest during the manifestation of a universe as regards that universe; it becomes latent in its dissolution.

In the All everything IS always; all that has been, all that now is manifest, all that will be, all that can be, all possibilities as well as all actualities, are ever in being in the All. That which is outwards, the forthgoing existence, the unfolded, is the manifested universe. That which IS as really, although inwards, the infolded, is the unmanifested universe. But the Within, the Unmanifested, is as real as the Without, the Manifested. The inter-relation between beings, in or out of manifestation, is the eternal karma. As Being never ceases, so karma never ceases, but always is. When part of that which is simultaneous in the All becomes manifested as a universe, the eternal inter-relation becomes successive, and is seen as cause and effect. In the one Being, the All, everything is linked to everything else, everything is related to everything else, and in the phenomenal, the manifested universe, these links and relations are drawn out into successive happenings, causally connected in the order of their succession in time, *i.e.*, in appearance.

Some students shrink from a metaphysical view such as this, but unless this idea of eternal Being, within which all beings ever are, is grasped, the centre cannot be reached. So long as we think from the circumference, there is always a question behind every answer, endless beginnings and endings with a "Why?" behind each beginning. If the student would escape this, he must patiently seek the centre, and let the concept of the All sink into his mind, until it becomes an ever-present part of his mental equipment, and then the universes on the circumference become intelligible, and the universal inter-relation between all things, seen from the simultaneity of the centre, naturally becomes cause and effect in the successions on the circumference. It has been said that the Eternal[1] is as an ocean, which throws up universes as waves. The ocean symbolizes being without form, ever the same. The wave, by virtue of being a part, has form and attributes. The waves rise and fall; they break into a foam, and the spray of the waves is as worlds in a universe.

Or we may think of a huge waterfall, like Niagara, where the mass of its torrent is one ere it falls, and then it divides into innumerable drops, which separately reflect the light; and the drops are as worlds, and the rainbow they make is the many-coloured life. But the water is one while the drops

[1] The Hindu name is Brahman, or more strictly, Nirguna Brahman, the Brahman without attributes.

are many, and, life is one though beings are many. God manifest or unmanifest is one and the same, though different, though showing attributes in manifestation, and attributeless in unmanifestation; the LOGOS and His universe are one, though He is the unity and the universe the diversity. He is the life and the universe the forms. Out of manifestation karma is latent, for the beings of the manifested are but concepts in the unmanifested; in manifestation karma is active, for all the parts of a world, of a system, of a universe, are inter-related. Science declares that no movement of a part can take place without affecting the whole, and scientifically all are agreed. The inter-relations are universal, and none can be broken, for the breaking of one would break the unity of the whole. The inviolability of natural law rests on its universality, and a breach of law in any part would mean universal chaos.

SUCCESSION

We have seen that as the manifestation of a universe implies succession of phenomena, so the universal inter-relation becomes the sequence of cause and effect. But each effect becomes in turn a cause, and so on endlessly, the difference between cause and effect being one not of nature but of relation. The inter-relations which exist in the thought of the Eternal become the inter-relations between phenomena in the manifested universe—the portion of the thought put forth as a universe. Before the manifestation of any special universe there will be, in the Eternal, the thought of the universe which is to be, and its inter-relations. That which exists simultaneously out of time and space, in the Eternal Now, gradually appears in time and space as successive phenomena. The moment you conceive a universe as made up of phenomena, you are obliged to think of these phenomena successively, one after another; but in the thought of the Eternal they always are, and the limitation of succession has there no existence.

Even in the lower worlds, where the measures of time are so different from each other, we catch a glimpse of the increasing limitations of denser matter. Mozart tells us of a state of unconsciousness in which he received a musical composition as a single impression, although in his waking consciousness he could only reproduce that single impression in a succession of notes. Or again, we may look at a picture, and receive a single mental impression—a landscape, a battle; but an ant, crawling over that picture, would see no whole, only successive impressions from the parts travelled over.

By simile, by analogy, we may gain some idea of the difference of a universe as it appears to the LOGOS and as it appears to us. To Him, a single impression, a perfect whole; to us an immense sequence, slowly unfolding. So what is to Him inter-relation becomes to us succession. Instead of seeing childhood, youth, old age, as a whole, we see them successively, day by day, year by year. That which is simultaneous and universal becomes successive and particular to our small minds, crawling over the world as the ant over the picture.

Go up a mountain and look down on a town, and you can see how the houses are related to each other in blocks, streets, and so on. You realize them as a whole. But when you go down into the town you must pass from street to street, seeing each separately, successively. So in karma, we see the relations only one by one, and one after another, not even realizing the successive relations, so limited is our view.

Such similes may often help us to grasp the invisible things, and may act as crutches to our halting imagination. And out of all this we lay our foundation-stone for our study of karma.

Karma is universal inter-relation, and is seen in any universe as the Law of Causation, in consequence of the successive appearance of phenomena in the becoming, or coming forth, of the universe.

CAUSATION

The idea of causation has been challenged in modern times, Huxley for instance contending, in the *Contemporary Review*, that we only know sequence, not causation; he said that if a ball moved after it was hit by a bat, you should not say that the blow of the bat caused the movement, but only that it was followed by the movement. This extreme scepticism came out strongly in some of the great men of the nineteenth century, a reaction from the ready credulity and many unproved assumptions of the Middle Ages. The reaction had its use, but is now gradually passing away, as extremes ever do.

The idea of causation arises naturally in the human mind, though unprovable by the senses; when a phenomenon has been invariably followed by another phenomenon for long periods of time, the two become linked together in our minds, and when one appears, the mind, by association of ideas, expects the second; thus the fact that night has been followed by day from time immemorial gives us a firm conviction that the sun will rise to-morrow as on countless yesterdays. Succession alone, however, does not necessarily imply causation; we do not regard day as the cause of night, nor night as the cause of day, because they invariably succeed each other. To assert causation we need more than invariable succession; we need that the reason shall see that which the senses are unable to discern —a *relation* between the two things which brings about the appearance of the second when the first appears. The succession of day and night is not caused by either; both are caused by the relation of the earth to the sun; that relation is a true cause, recognized as such by the reason, and as long as the relation exists unchanged, day and night will be its effect. In order to see one thing as the cause of another, the reason must establish a relation between them which is sufficient for the production of one by the other; then, and then only, can we rightly assert causation. The links between phenomena that are never broken, and that are recognized by the reason as an active relation, bringing into manifestation the second phenomenon whenever the first is manifested, we call causation. They are the shadows of inter-relations existing in the Eternal, outside space and time, and they extend over the life of a universe, wherever the conditions exist for their manifestation. Causation is an expression of the nature of the LOGOS, an emanation of the eternal Reality; wherever there is inter-relation in the Eternal which demands succession for its manifestation in time, *there* is causation.

The Laws of Nature

Our next step in our study is a consideration of the "Laws of Nature". The whole universe is included within the ideas of succession and causation, but when we come to what we call the laws of nature, we are unable to say over what area they extend. Scientists find themselves compelled to speak with greater and greater caution as they travel beyond the limit of actual observation. Causes and effects which are continuous within the area of our observation may not exist in other regions, or workings which are here observed as invariable may be interrupted by the irruption of some cause outside the "known" of our time, though probably not outside the knowable. Between 1850 and 1890 there were many positive statements as to the conservation of energy and the indestructibility of matter. It was said that there existed in the universe a certain amount of energy, incapable of diminution or of increase; that all forces were forms of that energy, and might be transmuted from one form to another; that the amount of any given force, as heat, might vary, but not the total amount of energy. As 20 may be made up of 20 units, or of 10 twos, or of 5 fours, or of 12+8, and so on, but the total remains as 20, so with the varying forms and the total amount. With regard to matter, again, similar statements were made; it was indestructible, and hence remained ever the same in amount; some, like Ludwig Buchner, declared that the chemical elements were indestructible, that "an atom of carbon was ever an atom of carbon," and so on.

On these two ideas science was built up, and they formed the basis of materialism. But now it is realized that chemical elements are dissoluble, and that the atom itself may be a swirl in the ether, or perhaps a mere hole where ether is not. There may be atoms through which force pours in, others through which it pours out—whence?—whither? May not physical matter become intangible, resolve itself into ether? May not ether give birth to new matter? All is doubtful where once certainty reigned. Yet has a universe its "Ring-Pass-Not". Within a given area only can we speak with certainty of a "law of nature".

What is a law of nature? Mr. J. N. Farquhar, in the *Contemporary Review* for July, 1910, in an article on Hinduism, declares that if Hindus want to carry out reforms, they must abandon the idea of karma. As well might he say that if a man wants to fly he must abandon the idea of an atmosphere. To understand the law of karma is not to renounce activity, but to know the conditions under which activity is best carried on. Mr. Farquhar, who has evidently studied *modern* Hinduism carefully, has not grasped the idea of karma as taught in ancient scripture and in modern science.

A law of nature is not a command, but a statement of conditions. This cannot be repeated too often, nor insisted on too strongly. Nature does not order this thing or the other; she says: "Here are certain conditions; where these exist, such and such a result will invariably follow." A law of nature is an invariable sequence. If you do not like the result, change the preceding conditions. Ignorant, you are helpless, at the mercy of nature's hurtling forces; wise, you are master, and her forces serve you obediently. Every law of nature is an enabling, not a compelling force, but knowledge is necessary for utilizing her powers.

Water boils at 100° C. under normal pressure. This is the condition. You go up a mountain; pressure diminishes; water boils at 95°. Now water at 95° will not make good tea. Does Nature then forbid you to have good tea on a mountain-top? Not at all; under normal pressure water boils at the necessary temperature for tea-making; you have lost pressure; supply the deficit; imprison your escaping steam till it adds the necessary pressure, and you can make your tea with water at 100°. If you want to produce water by the union of hydrogen and oxygen, you require a certain temperature, and can obtain it from the electric spark. If you insist on keeping the temperature at zero, or in substituting nitrogen for hydrogen, you cannot have water. Nature lays down the conditions which result in the production of water, and you cannot change them; she neither supplies nor withholds water; you are free to have it or to go without it; if you want it, you must bring together the necessary things and thus make the conditions. Without these, no water. With these, inevitably water. Are you bound or free? Free as to making the conditions; bound as to the result, when once you have made them. Knowing this, the scientific man, face to face with a difficulty, does not sit down helplessly; he finds out the conditions under which he can bring about a result, learns how to make the conditions, sure that he can rely on the result.

A Lesson of the Law

This is the great lesson taught by science to the present generation. Religion has taught it for ages, but dogmatically rather than rationally. Science proves that knowledge is the condition of freedom, and that only as man knows can he compel. The scientific man observes sequences; over and over again he performs his testing experiments; he eliminates all that is casual, collateral, irrelevant, and slowly, surely, discovers what constitutes an invariable causative sequence. Once sure of his facts, he acts with indubitable assurance, and nature, without shadow of turning, rewards his rational certainty with success.

Out of this assurance grows "the sublime patience of the investigator". Luther Burbank, in California, will sow millions of seeds, select some thousands of plants, pair a few hundreds, and patiently march to his end; he can trust the laws of nature, and if he fails he knows that the error lies with him, not with them.

There is a law of nature that masses of matter tend to move towards the earth. Shall I then say: "I cannot walk up the stairs; I cannot fly in the air"? Nay, there are other laws. I pit against the force that holds me on the ground another force stored in my muscles, and I raise my body by means of it. A person with muscles weak from fever may have to stay on the ground-floor, helpless; but I break no law when I put forth muscular force and walk upstairs.

The inviolability of Law does not bind—it frees. It makes Science possible, and rationalizes human effort. In a lawless universe, effort would be futile, reason would be useless. We should be savages, trembling in the grip of forces, strange, incalculable, terrible. Imagine a chemist in a laboratory where nitrogen was now inert, now explosive, where oxygen vivified to-day and stifled to-morrow! In a lawless universe we should not dare to move, not knowing what any action might bring about. We move safely, surely, because of the inviolability of Law.

Karma does not Crush

Now Karma is the great law of nature, with all that that implies. As we are able to move in the physical universe with security, knowing its laws, so may we move in the mental and moral universes with security also, as we learn their laws. The majority of people, with regard to their mental and moral defects, are much in the position of a man who should decline to walk upstairs because of the law of gravitation. They sit down helplessly, and say: "That is my nature. I cannot help it." True, it *is* the man's nature, as he has made it in the past, and it *is* "his karma". But by a knowledge of karma he can change his nature, making it other to-morrow than it is to-day. He is not in the grip of an inevitable destiny, imposed upon him from outside; he is in a world of law, full of natural forces which he can utilize to bring about the state of things which he desires. Knowledge and will—that is what he needs. He must realize that karma is not a power which crushes, but a statement of conditions out of which invariable results accrue. So long as he lives carelessly, in a happy-go-lucky way, so long will he be like a man floating on a stream, struck by any passing log, blown aside by any casual breeze, caught in any chance eddy. This spells failure, misfortune, unhappiness. The law enables him to compass his ends successfully, and places within his reach forces which he can utilize. He can modify, change, remake on other lines the nature which is the inevitable outcome of his previous desires, thoughts and actions; that future nature is as inevitable as the present, the result of the conditions which he now deliberately makes. "Habit is second nature," says the proverb, and thought creates habits. Where there is Law, no achievement is impossible, and karma is the guarantee of man's evolution into mental and moral perfection.

We have now to apply this law to ordinary human life, to apply principle to practice. It has been the loss of the intelligible relations between eternal principles and transitory events that has rendered modern religion so inoperative in common life. A man will clean up his back-yard when he understands the relation between dirt and disease; but he leaves his mental and moral back-yards uncleansed, because he sees no relation between his mental and moral defects and the various ghastly after-death experiences with which he is threatened by religions. Hence he either disbelieves the threats and goes carelessly on his way, or hopes to escape consequences by some artificial compact with the authorities. In either case, he does not cleanse his ways. When he realizes that law is as inviolable in the mental and moral worlds as in the physical, it may well be hoped that he will become as reasonable in the former as he already is in the latter.

Man in the Three Worlds

Man, as we know, is living normally in three worlds, the physical, emotional and mental, is put into contact with each by a body formed of its type of matter, and acts in each through the appropriate body. He therefore creates results in each according to their respective laws and powers, and all these come within the all-embracing law of karma. During his daily life in waking consciousness he is creating "karma," *i.e.*, results, in these three worlds, by action, desire and thought. While his physical body is asleep, he is creating karma in two worlds —the emotional and the mental—the amount of karma then created by him depending on the stage he has reached in evolution.

We may confine ourselves to these three worlds, for those above them are not inhabited consciously by the average man; but we should, none the less, remember that we are like trees, the roots of which are fixed in the higher worlds, and their branches spread in the three lower worlds in which dwell our mortal bodies, and in which our consciousnesses are working.

Laws work within their own worlds, and must be studied as though their workings were independent. Just as every science studies the laws working within its own department, but does not forget the wider working of further-reaching conditions, so must man, while working in the three departments, physical, emotional and mental, remember the sweep of law which includes them all within its area of activity. In all departments laws are inviolable and unchangeable, and each brings about its own full effects, although the final result of their interaction is the effective force that remains when all balancing of opposing forces has been made. All that is true of laws in general is true of karma, the great law. Causes being present, events must follow. But by taking away or adding causes, events must be modified.

A person gets drunk; may he say: "My karma is to get drunk"? He gets drunk because of certain tendencies existing in himself, the presence of loose companions, and an environment where drink is sold. Let us suppose that he wishes to conquer his evil habit; he knows the three conditions that lead him into drunkenness. He may say: "I am not strong enough to resist my own tendencies in the presence of drink and the company of loose-livers. I will not go where there is drink, nor will I associate with men who tempt me to drink." He changes the conditions, eliminating two of them, though unable immediately to change the third, and the new result is that he does not get drunk. He is not "interfering with karma," but is relying on it; nor is a friend "interfering with karma," if he persuades him to keep away from boon companions. There is no karmic command to a man to get drunk, but only the existence of certain conditions in the midst of which he certainly will get drunk; there is, it is true, another way of changing the conditions, the putting forth of a strong effort of will; this also introduces a new condition, which will change the result—by addition instead of elimination.

In the only sense in which a man can "interfere" with the laws of nature he is perfectly at liberty to do so, as much as he likes and can. He can inhibit the acting of one force by bringing another against it; he can overcome gravitation by muscular effort. In this sense, he may interfere with karma as much as he likes, and should interfere with it when the results are objectionable. But the expression is not a happy one, and it is liable to be misunderstood.

The law is: such and such causes bring about such and such results. The law is unchangeable, but the play of phenomena is ever-changing. The mightiest cause of all causes is human will and human reason, and yet this is the cause which is, for the most part, omitted when people talk of karma. *We* are causes, because we are the divine will, one with God in our essential being, although hampered by ignorance and working through gross matter, which impedes us until we conquer by spiritualizing it. The changelessness of karma is not the changelessness of effects but of law, and it is this which makes us free. Truly slaves should we be in a world in which everything went by chance. But according to our knowledge are our freedom and our safety in a world of law. In the Middle Ages, chemists were by no means free to bring about the results they desired, but they had to accept results as they came, unforeseen and for the most part undesired, even to their own serious injury. The result of an experiment might be a useful product, or it might be the reduction of the experimenter into fragments. Roger Bacon set going causes which cost him an eye and a finger, and occasionally stretched him senseless on the floor of his cell; outside our knowledge we are in peril, and any cause we set going may wreck us, for we are mostly Roger Bacons in the mental and moral worlds; inside our knowledge we may move with freedom and safety, as the well-trained chemist moves to-day. It is true in all the three worlds in which we live that the more we know, the more can we foresee and control. Because law is inviolable and changeless, therefore knowledge is the condition of freedom. Let us then study karma, and apply our knowledge to the guidance of our lives. So many people say: "Oh! how I wish I were good," and do not use the law to create the causes which result in goodness; as though a chemist should say: "Oh! how I wish I had water," without making the conditions which would produce it.

Again, we must remember that each force works along its own particular line, and that when a number of forces impinge on a particular point, the resultant force is the outcome of all of them. As in our school days we learned how to construct a parallelogram of forces and thus find the resultant of their composition, so with karma may we learn to understand the conflict of forces and their composition to yield a single resultant. We hear people asking why a good man fails in business while a bad man succeeds. But there is no causal connection between goodness and moneygetting. We might as well say: "I am a very good man;

why cannot I fly in the air?" Goodness is not a cause of flying, nor does it bring in money. Tennyson touched on a great law when, in his poem on "Wages," he declared that the wages of virtue were not "dust," nor rest, nor pleasure, but the glory of an active immortality. "Virtue is its own reward," in the fullest sense of the words. If we are truthful, our reward is that our nature becomes more truthful, and so sequentially with every virtue. Karmic results can only be of the nature of their causes; they are not arbitrary, like human rewards.

Understand the Truth

This seems to be obvious; whence then arises the general instinct that success in life should accompany goodness? We can successfully combat an error only when we understand the truth which lies at the heart of it, gives it its vitality, and leads to its spread and its persistence. The truth in this case is that, if a man puts himself into accord with the divine law, happiness is the result of such harmony. The error is to identify worldly success with happiness and to disregard the element of time. A man going into business determines to be truthful, and to take no unfair advantage over others. He sees those who are untruthful and unscrupulous going ahead of him; if he is weak, he becomes discouraged, even, perchance, imitates them. If he is strong, he says: "I will work in harmony with the divine law, no matter what may be the immediate worldly results"; inner peace and happiness are then his, but success does not accrue to him; nevertheless, in the long run even that may fall to him, for what he loses in money he gains in confidence, whereas the man who once betrays may at any time betray again, and none will trust him. In a competitive society, lack of scrupulousness yields immediate success, whereas in a co-operative society conscientiousness would "pay". To give starvation wages to workers forced by competition to accept them may lead to immediate success as against business rivals, and the man who gives a decent living wage may find himself outpaced in the race for wealth; but in the long run the latter will have better work done for him, and in the future will reap the harvest of happiness whereof he sowed the seed. We must decide on our course and accept its results, not looking for money as payment for goodness, nor seeing injustice when unscrupulous shrewdness reaches that at which it aimed.

An instructive, if not very pleasant, Indian story is told of a man who wronged another, and the injured man cried for redress to the King. When the punishment to be inflicted on his enemy was given into his hands, he prayed the King to enrich his foe ; asked for the reason of his strange behaviour, he grimly said that wealth and worldly prosperity would give him greater opportunities for wrong-doing, and would thus entail on him bitter suffering in the life after death. Often the worst enemy of virtue is in easy material conditions, and these, which are spoken of as good karma, are often the reverse in their results. Many who do fairly well in adversity go astray in prosperity, and become intoxicated with worldly delights.

Let us now consider how a man affects his surroundings, or in scientific phrase, how the organism acts on its environment.

Man affects his surroundings in innumerable ways, which may all be classified into three modes of Self-expression: he affects them by Will, by Thought, by Action.

The developed man is able to draw his energies together and to fuse them into one, ready to go forth from him and to cause action. This concentration of his energies into a single force, held in suspense within him in leash ready for outrush, is Will ; it is an interior concentration, one mode of the triple Self-expression. In the sub-human kingdoms, and in the lower divisions of the human, the pleasure-giving and pain-giving objects around the living creature draw out its energies, and we call these multifarious energies brought out by external objects its desires, whether of attraction or repulsion. Only when these are all drawn in, united and pointed towards a single aim, can we term this single energy, ready to go forth, the Will. This Will is *Self*-expression, *i.e.*, it is directed by the Self; the Self determines the line to be taken, basing its determination on previous experience. In the subhuman and lower human kingdoms, desires are an important factor in karma, giving rise to most mixed results; in the higher human Will is the most potent karmic cause, and as man transmutes desires into Will, he "rules his stars".

The mode of Self-expression called Thought belongs to the aspect of the Self by which he becomes aware of the outer world, the aspect of Cognition. This obtains knowledge, and the working of the Self on the knowledge obtained is Thought. This, again, is an important factor in karma, since it is creative and, as we know, builds character.

The mode of Self-expression which directly affects the environment, the energy going forth from the Self, is Activity, the action of the Self on the Not-Self. The power of concentrating all energies into one is Will; the power of becoming aware of an external world is Cognition; the power of affecting that outside world is Activity. This action is inevitably followed by a reaction from the outside world —karma. The inner cause of the reaction is Will;

the nature of the reaction is due to Cognition; the immediate provoker of the reaction is Activity. These spin the three threads of the karmic rope.

The Three Fates

"God created man in His own image," says a Hebrew Scripture, and the Trinities of the great religions are the symbols of the three aspects of the divine consciousness, reflected in the triplicity of the human. The First Logos of the Theosophist, the Mahādeva of the Hindu, the Father of the Christian, has Will as predominant, and shows forth the power of sovereignty, the Law by which the universe is built. The Second Logos, Vishnu, the Son, is Wisdom, that all-sustaining and all-pervading power by which the universe is preserved. The Third Logos, Brahmā, the Holy Spirit, is the Agent, the creative power by which the universe is brought into manifestation. There is nothing in divine or human consciousness which does not find itself within one or other of these modes of Self-expression.

Again, matter has three fundamental qualities responsive severally to these modes of consciousness, and without these it could no more be manifested than consciousness could express itself without its modes. It has inertia (tamas), the very foundation of all, the stability necessary to existence, the quality which answers to Will. It has mobility (rajas), the capacity to be moved, answering to Activity. It has rhythm (sattva), the equalizer of movement (without which movement would be chaotic, destructive), answering to Cognition. The Yoga system, considering all from the standpoint of consciousness, names this rhythmic quality "cognizability," that which makes that matter should be known by Spirit.

All that is in our consciousness, affecting the environment, and all the environment affected by our consciousness, make up our world. The inter-relation between our consciousness and our environment is our karma. By these three modes of consciousness we spin our individual karma, the universal inter-relation between Self and Not-Self being specialized by us into this individual inter-relation. As we rise above separateness, the individual again becomes the universal inter-relation, but this universal inter-relation cannot be transcended while manifestation endures. This specializing of the universal, and the later universalizing of the special make up the "world's eternal ways" —the Path of Forthgoing to gather experience, the Path of Return, bringing the sheaves of experience home; this is the Great Wheel of Evolution, so relentless when seen from the standpoint of Matter, so beauteous when seen from the standpoint of Spirit. "Life is not a cry, but a song."

THE PAIR OF TRIPLETS

Thus we have three factors in spirit for the creation of Karma, and three corresponding qualities in matter, and we must study these in order to make our Karma that which we would have it be. We may study them in any order, but for many reasons it is convenient to take the cognitive factor first, because in that lies the power of knowledge and of choice. We can change our desires by the use of thought; we cannot change our thoughts, though we may colour them, by desire; so in the final analysis action is set in motion by thought.

In the earliest stages of savagery, as with the newly born infant, action is caused by attractions and repulsions. But almost immediately memory comes in, the memory of an attraction with the wish to re-experience it; the memory of a repulsion with the wish to avoid it. A thing has given pleasure; it is remembered, *i.e.*, thought about; it is desired, action to grasp it follows. The three cannot really be separated, for there is no action which is not preceded by thought and desire, and which does not again set them going, after it is performed.

Action is the outer sign of the invisible thought and desire, and in its very accomplishment gives birth to a fresh thought and desire. The three form a circle, perpetually retraced.

Thought, the Builder

Now thought works on matter; every change in consciousness is answered by a vibration in matter, and a similar change, however often repeated, brings a similar vibration. This vibration is strongest in the matter nearest to you, and the matter nearest to you is your own mental body. If you repeat a thought, it repeats the corresponding vibration; and, as when matter has vibrated in a particular way once it is easier for it to vibrate in that same way again than to vibrate in a new way, the more often you repeat a thought the more ready the vibrationary response. Presently, after much repetition, a tendency will be set up in the matter of your mental body, automatically to repeat the vibration on its own account; when it does this—since the vibration in matter and the thought in consciousness are inseparably linked—the thought appears in the mind without any previous activity on the part of consciousness.

Hence when you have thought over a thing—a virtue, an emotion, a wish—and have deliberately come to the conclusion that it is a desirable thing to have that virtue, to feel that emotion, to be moved by that wish, you quietly set to work to create a habit of thought.

You think deliberately of it every morning for a few minutes, and soon you find that it arises spontaneously in the mind (by the aforesaid automatic activity of matter). You persist in your thought-creation until you have formed a strong habit of thought, a habit which can only be changed by an equally prolonged process of thinking in the opposite direction. Even against the opposition of the will the thought recurs to the mind—as many have found when they are unable to sleep in consequence of the involuntary recurrence of a harassing thought. If you have thus established the habit, say, of honesty, you will automatically act honestly; and if some strong gust of desire sweeps you into dishonesty on some occasion, the honest habit will torment you as it would never torment a habitual thief. You have created the habit of honesty; the thief has no such habit; hence you suffer mentally when the habit is broken, and the thief suffers not at all. Persistence in strengthening such a mental habit until it is stronger than any force which can be brought to bear upon it makes the reliable man; he literally *cannot* lie, *cannot* steal; he has built himself an impregnable virtue.

By thought, then, you can build any habit you choose to build. There is no virtue which you cannot create by thought. The forces of nature work with you, for you understand how to use them, and they become your servants.

If you love your husband, your wife, your child, you find that this emotion of love causes happiness in those who feel it. If you spread the love outwards to others, an increase of happiness results. You, seeing this and wishful for the happiness of all, deliberately begin to think love to others, in an ever wider and wider circle, until the love-attitude is your normal attitude towards all you meet. You have created the love-habit, and have generalized an emotion into a virtue, for a virtue is only a good emotion made general and permanent.[1]

Everything is under law; you cannot obtain mental ability or moral virtue by sitting still and doing nothing. You can obtain both by strenuous and persevering thought. You can build your mental and moral nature by thinking, for "man is created by thought; what he thinks upon, that he becomes; therefore think" on that which you aspire to be, and inevitably it shall be yours. Thus shall you become a mental and moral athlete, and your character shall grow rapidly; you made in the past

[1] See *The Science of the Emotions* by Bhagavan Das.

the character with which you were born; you are making now the character with which you will die, *and will return.* This is karma. Every one is born with a character, and the character is the most important part of karma. The Mussalman says that "a man is born with his destiny tied round his neck". For a man's destiny depends chiefly on his character. A strong character can overcome the most unfavourable circumstances, and overclimb the most difficult obstacles. A weak character is buffeted by circumstances, and fails before the most trivial obstacles.

Practical Meditation

The whole theory of meditation is built upon these laws of thought; for meditation is only deliberate and persevering thought, aimed at a specific object, and hence is a potent karmic cause. By using knowledge and thought to modify character, you can bring about very quickly a desired result. If you were born a coward, you can think yourself brave; if you were born dishonest, you can think yourself honest; if you were born untruthful, you can think yourself truthful. Have confidence in yourself and in the law. There is another point we must not forget. Concrete thought finds its natural realization in action, and if you do not act out a thought, then by reaction you weaken the thought. Strenuous action along the line of the thinking must follow the thought, otherwise progress will be slow.

Realize, then, that while you cannot now help the character with which you were born, while it is a fact which must profoundly influence your present destiny, marking out your line of activity in this life, yet you can, by thought and by action based thereon, change your inborn character, eliminate its weaknesses, eradicate its faults, strengthen its good qualities, enlarge its capacities. You are born with a given character, but you can change it. Knowledge is offered to you as to the means of changing, and each must put that knowledge into practice for himself.

Will and Desire

Desire and Activity remain to be considered. Will is the energy prompting to action, and while it is attracted and repelled by outside objects, we call it desire, the lower aspect of Will, as thought is the lower aspect of Cognition. If a man, confronted by a pleasure-giving object, grasps it without thought, he is moved by desire; if he holds himself back, saying: "I must not enjoy it now, because I have a duty to perform," he is moved by Will. When the energy of the Self is controlled and guided by right reason, it is Will; when it rushes out unbridled, drawn hither and thither by attractive objects, it is Desire.

Desire arises in us spontaneously; we like one thing, we dislike another, and our likes and dislikes are involuntary, are not under the control of the Will or of the reason. We may make up reasons for them when we wish to justify them, but they are elemental, non-rational, precedent of thought. None the less may they be brought under control and changed—though not directly.

Consider physical taste; an olive, preserved in brine, is offered to a child, and is generally rejected with disgust. But it is a fashionable thing to like olives, and young people persevere in eating them, determined to like them, and presently they are fond of them. They have changed their disliking into liking. How is the change of taste brought about? By the action of Will, directed by the mind.

The Mastery of Desire

We can change desires by thought. The desire-nature with which we are born is good, bad, or indifferent, and it follows its own way in early childhood. Presently we examine it, and mark some desires as useful, others as useless or even noxious.

We then form a mental image of the desire-nature which would be useful and noble, and we deliberately set to work to create it by thought-power. There are some physical desires which we see will bring about disease if left uncontrolled: eating too much because of the gratification of the palate; drinking alcoholic liquors, because they exhilarate and vivify; yielding to the pleasures of sex. We see in the persons of others that these cause obesity, shaken nerves, premature exhaustion. We determine not to yield to them; we bridle the horses of the senses with the bits and reins of the mind, and deliberately hold them in, although they struggle; if they are very refractory we call up the image of the glutton, the drunkard, the worn-out profligate, and so create a repulsion for the causes which made them what they are. And so with all other desires. Deliberately choose out and encourage those which lead to refining and elevating pleasures, and reject those which result in coarseness of body and of mind. There will be failures in your resistance, but in spite of failures, persevere. At first you will yield to the desire and only remember too late that you had resolved to abstain; persevere. Presently the desire and the memory of the good resolution will arise together, and there will be a period of struggle—your Kurukshetra—and you will sometimes succeed and sometimes fail; persevere. Then successes will multiply, and failures be few; persevere. Then desire dies, and you watch beside its tomb, lest it should only be entranced, and revive. Finally you have done with that form of desire for ever. You have worked with the law and have conquered.

Two Other Points

1. Students are sometimes troubled because in their dreams they yield to a vice which down here they have conquered, or feel the stirring of a desire which they thought long slain. Knowledge will destroy the trouble. In a dream, a man is in his astral body, and a stirring of desire, too weak to cause physical matter to vibrate, will cause a vibration in astral matter; let the dreamer resist, as he soon will if he determines to do so, and the desire will cease. Further, he should remember that there will be left for some time in the astral body effete matter, which was formerly used when the desire arose, but which is now, from disuse, in process of disintegration. This may be temporarily vivified by a passing desire-form and thus caused to vibrate artificially. This may happen to a man when he is either sleeping or waking. It is but the artificial movement of a corpse. Let him repudiate it: "Thou art not from me. Get thee gone." And the vibration will be stilled.

2. The warrior who is battling with desire must not let his mind dwell on the objects which arouse desire. Again, thought is creative. Thought will awaken desire, and stir it into vigorous activity. Of the man who abstained from action but enjoyed in thought, Shri Krishna sternly said: "That deluded man is called a hypocrite." Nourished by thought, desires cannot die. They will but become stronger by physical repression when fed by thought. It is better not to fight desire, but rather to evade it. If it arises, turn the mind to something else, to a book, a game, to anything which is at once pure and attractive. By fighting it, the mind dwells on it, and thus feeds and strengthens it. If you know that the desire is likely to arise, have ready something to which to turn *at once*. So shall it be starved out, having no nourishment of either act or thought.

Never let us forget that objects are desirable because of the immanence of God. "There is nothing moving or unmoving that can exist bereft of Me." At a certain stage of evolution, the attraction to them makes for progress. Only later on are they superseded. The child plays with a doll; it is well; it draws out the germinal mother-love. But a grown woman playing with a doll would be pitiable. Objects of desire draw out emotions which aid in development and stimulate exertion. They cease to be useful when we have grown beyond them, and in ceasing to be useful they become mischievous.

The bearing of all this on karma is self-evident. Since by desire we create opportunities and attract within our reach the objects of desire, our desires now map out our opportunities and our possessions hereafter. By harbouring none but pure desires and wishing for naught that cannot be used in service, we ensure a future of opportunities for helping our fellows, and of possessions which shall be consecrated to the Master's work.

The Third Thread

We have now to consider how karma works in relation to activity, the third aspect of the Self. Our activities—the ways in which we affect the outer world of matter—spin the third thread of our karma, and in many respects this is the least important. Our thoughts and our desires, so soon as they flow outwards, by producing vibrations in the mental and astral matter surrounding us, or by creating specific thought-forms and desire-forms, become activities, are our action on the outer worlds of life and form, of consciousness and bodies. The moment they speed outwards they affect other things and other people, they are the action, or the reaction, as the case may be, of the organism on the environment. The reaction of our thoughts on ourselves, as we have seen, is the building of character and of faculty; the reaction of our desires on ourselves is the gaining of opportunities and objects and of power; the reaction of our activities on ourselves is our environment, the conditions and circumstances, the friends and enemies, that surround us. The nearest circumstance, the expression of part of our past activities, is our physical body; this is shaped for us by an elemental specially created for the task; our body is nature's answer to such part of the sum of our past activities as can be expressed in a single material form, and "nature" is here the Lords of Karma, the mighty Angels of Judgment, the Recorders of the Past. Two parts of karma we bring with us—our thought-nature and our desire-nature, the germinal tendencies we have created in our age-long past. The third part of karma we are born into, that which limits our Self-expression and constrains us; our past action on the external world reacts upon us as the sum of our limitations—our environment, including our physical body.

It is probable that a close study of past activities and present environment would result in a knowledge of details that at present we do not possess. We read in Buddhist and Hindu Scriptures a mass of details on this subject, probably drawn from meticulous careful observation. At present, we modern students can only affirm a few broad facts. Extreme cruelty inflicted on the helpless—on heretics, on children, on animals—reacts on inquisitors, on brutal parents and teachers, on vivisectors, as physical deformity, more or less revolting and extreme, according to the nature and extent of the cruelty.

Perfect Justice

From the physical agony inflicted results physical agony endured, for karma is the restoration of the equilibrium disturbed. Motive, in this region, does not mitigate, any more than the pain of a burn is mitigated because the injury has been sustained in saving a child from the fire. Where a good motive existed, however intellectually misdirected—as the saving of souls from the torture of hell in the case of the inquisitor, or the saving of bodies from the torture of disease in the case of the vivisector—it has its full result in the region of character. Hence we may find a person born deformed, with a gentle and patient character, showing that in a past life he strove to see the right and did the wrong. The Angels of Judgment are utterly just, and the golden thread of completely misdirected love may gleam beside the black thread woven by cruelty; none the less will the black thread draw to the doer of cruelty a misshapen body. On the other hand, where lust of power and indifference to the pain of others have mingled their baleful influences with the infliction of cruelty, there will be found also a mental and emotional twist; a historical case is that of Marat, who, instead of expiating the cruelty of the past, intensified it by new cruelty in the very life in which he was reaping the harvest of previous evil. Hereditary and congenital diseases again are the reaction from past misdeeds. The drunkard of a previous life will be born into a family in which drunkenness has left diseases of the nerves—epilepsy and the like. The profligate will be born into a family tainted with diseases which spring from sexual vice. A "bad heredity" is the reaction from wrong activities in the past. Often the man who is reaping these sad harvests shows in his moral nature that he has purged himself from the evil, though the physical harvesting remains. A steadfast patience, a sweet enduring content, tell that the evil lies behind, that victory has been gained, though the wounds sustained in the conflict smart and sting. So may a soldier, sorely maimed in a fierce battle, remain mutilated for the rest of his physical life, and yet not regret with any keenness the anguish and the loss which mark that he has gloriously discharged his duty to his flag. And these warriors who have conquered in a greater battle need not lament too bitterly over the weakness or deformity of a body which tells of a strife which is past, but may wear patiently the badge of a struggle with an evil they have overcome, knowing that in another life no scar of that struggle shall remain.

Our Environment

The nation and the family into which a man is born give him the field suitable for the development of faculties he needs, or for the exercise of faculties he has gained, which are required for the helping of others at that place and time. Sometimes a strenuous life passed in the company of superiors, which has stimulated latent powers and quickened the growth of germinal faculties, is followed by one of ease amid ordinary people, in order to test the reality of the strength acquired and the solidity of the apparent conquest over self. Sometimes, when an ego has definitely gained certain mental faculties and has secured them as part of his mental equipment by sufficient practice, he will be born into surroundings where these are useless, and confronted by tasks of a most uncongenial nature. A man ignorant of karma will fret and fume, will perform grudgingly his distasteful duties, and will think regretfully of his " wasted talents, while that fool Jones is in a place which he is not fit to fill " ; he does not realize Jones has to learn a lesson which he himself has already mastered, and that he himself would not be evolving further by repeating over again that which he has already done. In a similar situation, the knower of karma will quietly study his surroundings, will realize that he would gain nothing by doing that which it would be easy for him to do—*i.e.*, that which he has already done well in the past—and will address himself contentedly to the uncongenial work, seeking to understand what it has to teach him, and resolutely setting himself to learn the new lesson.

Our Kith and Kin

So also with an ego who finds himself entangled with family responsibilities and duties, when he would fain spring forward to answer a call for helpers in a larger work. If ignorant of karma, he will fret against his bonds, or even break them, and thus ensure their return in the future. The knower of karma will see in these duties the reactions from his own past activities, and will patiently accept and discharge them; he knows that when they are fully paid, they will drop away from him and leave him free, and that meanwhile they have some lessons to teach him which it is incumbent upon him to learn; he will seek to see those lessons and to learn them, sure that the powers they evoke will make him a more efficient helper when he is free to answer to the call to which his whole nature is thrilling in response.

Again, the knower of karma will seek to establish, in his nation and his family, conditions which will attract to each egos of an advanced and noble type. He will see to it that his household arrangements, its scrupulous cleanliness, its hygienic conditions, its harmony, good feeling, and loving-kindness, the purity of its mental and moral atmosphere, shall form a magnet of attraction, drawing towards it and into relationship with it egos of a high level, whether they be seeking embodiment—if young parents are members of the household—or be already in bodies, coming into the family as future husbands and wives, friends, or dependants. So far as his power extends, he will help in forming similar conditions in his town, his province, his country. He knows that egos must be born amid surroundings suitable for them, and that, therefore, by providing good surroundings he will attract egos of desirable type.

OUR NATION

With regard to national environment, the knower of karma must carefully study the national conditions into which he is born, in order to see whether he is born therein chiefly to develop qualities in which he is deficient, or chiefly to help his nation by qualities well developed in himself. In times of transition many egos may be born into a nation, with qualities of the type required in the new conditions into which that nation is passing. Thus, in America, which will presently develop the beginnings of a Commonwealth in which co-operation shall replace competition, there have been born a number of egos of vast organizing ability, of highly developed will-power, and of keen commercial intelligence; they have created Trusts, organizations of industry built with consummate ability, manifesting the economical advantages of doing away with competition, of controlling production and supply, of meeting, but not over-meeting, demand. They have thus opened the way to co-operative production and distribution, and prepared for a happier future. Soon will be born the egos who will see in the securing of the comfort of the nation a greater stimulus than personal gain, and *they* will complete the transition process; the one set have gathered into a head the forces of individualism; the other set will bend these forces to the common good.

Thus is environment governed by karma, and by a knowledge of law the desired environment may be created. If it grips us when once called into being, it is none the less ours to decide what that being shall be. Our power over that future environment is now in our hands, for its creator is the activities of the present.

Here is

The Light for a Good Man

who finds himself surrounded by unhappy conditions. He has made his character, and he has also made his circumstances. His good thoughts and desires have made him what he is; the misdirection of them has created the environment through which he suffers. Let him, then, not be satisfied with being good, but see to it also that his influence on all around him is beneficial. Then shall it react on him as good environment. For instance: a mother is very unselfish, and she spoils her son by yielding, at her own cost, to all his whims, aiding him not at all to overcome his own selfish inclinations, fostering the lower nature, starving the higher. The son grows up selfish, uncontrolled, the slave of his own whims and desires. He causes unhappiness in the home, perchance brings upon it debt and disgrace. This reaction is the environment she created by her unwisdom, and she must bear the distresses it brings upon her.

A selfish man may, on the other hand, create for himself in the future an environment regarded as fortunate by the world. With the hope of gaining a title, he builds a hospital and equips it fully; many sufferers therein find relief, many sick unto death have their last moments soothed, many children are lovingly nursed back into health. The reaction from all this will be easy and pleasant surroundings for himself; he will reap the harvest of the physical good which he has sown. But his selfishness will also sow according to its kind, and mentally and morally he will reap that harvest also, a harvest of disappointment and of pain.

KNOWLEDGE OF LAW

The knowledge of karma will not only enable a man to build, as he wills, his own future, but it will also enable him to understand the workings of karmic law in the cases of others, and thus more effectively to help them. Only by knowledge of law can we move fearlessly and usefully in worlds where law is inviolable, and, secure ourselves, enable others to reach a similar security. In the physical world the supremacy of law is universally admitted, and the man who disregards 'natural law' is regarded not as a criminal but as a fool. Equal is the folly, and more far-reaching, of disregarding "natural law" in the worlds above the physical, and of imagining that, while law in the physical world is omnipresent, the mental and moral worlds are lawless and disorderly. In those worlds, as in the physical, law is inviolable and omnipresent, and of all is it true:

> Though the mills of God grind slowly, yet they grind exceeding small;
> Though with patience He stands waiting, with exactness grinds He all.

We have seen that our present is the outcome of our past, that by thought we have built our character, by desires our opportunities of satisfying them, by actions our environment. Let us now consider how far we can modify in the present these results of our past, how far we are compelled, how far we are free.

Two Opposing Schools

In the thought of the outer world, quite apart from the ideas of reincarnation and karma, there has been much opposing opinion. Robert Owen and his school regarded man as the creation of circumstances, ignoring heredity, that faint scientific reflection of karma; they considered that by changing the environment the man could be changed, most effectively if the child were taken ere he had formed bad habits; a child taken out of evil surroundings and placed amid good ones would grow into a good man. The failure of Robert Owen's great social experiment showed that his theory did not contain all the truth. Others, realizing the force of heredity, almost ignored environment; "Nature," said Ludwig Buchner, "is stronger than nurture." In both these extreme views there is truth. Inasmuch as the child brings with him the nature built in his past, but dons the garments of a new mentality and a new emotional nature, in which his self-created faculties and qualities exist indeed, but as germs, not as fully developed powers, these germs may be nourished into rapid growth or atrophied by lack of nourishment, and this is wrought by the influence of the environment for good or ill. Moreover, the child puts on also the garment of a new physical body, with its own physical heredity, designed for the expression of some of the powers he brings with him, and this can be largely affected by his environment, and developed healthily or unhealthily. These facts were on the side of Robert Owen's theory, and they explain the successes gained by such philanthropic institutions as Dr. Barnardo's Homes, wherein germs of good are cultured and germs of evil are starved out. But the congenital criminal, and beings of that ilk, none may redeem in a single life, and these, of various grades, are the non-successes of the benevolent rescuer.

Equally true is it, as the opposite school affirmed, that inborn character is a force with which every educationalist must reckon; he cannot create faculties which are not there; he cannot wholly eradicate evil tendencies which, below the surface, throw out roots, seeking appropriate nourishment; some nourishment reaches them from the thought-atmosphere around, from the evil desire-forms which arise from the evil in others, forms of thoughts and desires which float in the air around, and cannot wholly be shut out—save by occult means, unknown to the ordinary educationalist.

The More Modern View

The more modern scientific view that organism and environment act and react upon each other, each modifying the other, and that from the modifications new actions and reactions arise, and so on perpetually, takes in that which is true in each of the earlier views; it only needs to be expanded by the recognition of an enduring consciousness passing from life to life bringing its past with it, ever-growing, ever-evolving, and with its growth and evolution becoming an ever more and more potent factor in the direction and control of its future destiny.

Thus we reach the Theosophic standpoint; we cannot now help that which we have brought with us, nor can we help the environment into which we have been thrown; but we can modify both, and the more we know, the more effectively can we modify.

SELF-EXAMINATION

The first step is deliberately to examine what we may call our "stock in trade"; our inborn faculties and qualities, good and bad, our powers and our weaknesses, our present opportunities, our actual environment. Our character is that which is most rapidly modifiable, and on this we should set to work, selecting the qualities which it is desirable to strengthen, the weaknesses which form our most pressing dangers. We take them one by one, and use our thought-power in the way before described, remembering always that we must never think of the weakness but of its corresponding power. We think that which we desire to be, and gradually, inevitably, we become it. The law cannot fail; we have only to work with it in order to succeed.

The desire-nature is similarly modified by thought, and we create the thought-forms of the opportunities we need; alert to see and to grasp a suitable opportunity, our will also fixes itself on the forms our thought creates, and thus draws them within reach, literally making and then grasping the opportunities which the karma of the past does not present to us.

Hardest of all to change is our environment, for here we are dealing with the densest form of matter, that on which our thought-force is least potent. Here our freedom is very restricted, for we are at our weakest and the past is at its strongest. Yet are we not wholly helpless, for here, either by struggling or by yielding, we can conquer in the end. Such undesirable part of our surroundings as we can change by strenuous effort, we promptly set to work to change; that which we cannot thus change, we accept, and set ourselves to learn whatever it has to teach. When we have learnt its lesson, it will drop away from us like an outworn garment. We have an undesirable family; well, these are the egos we have drawn around us by our past; we fulfil every obligation cheerfully and patiently, honourably paying our debts; we acquire patience through the annoyances they inflict on us, fortitude through their daily irritations, forgiveness through their wrongs. We use them as a sculptor uses his tools, to chip off our excrescences and to smooth and polish away our roughnesses. When their usefulness to us is over, they will be removed by circumstances, carried off elsewhere. And so with other parts of our environment which, on the surface, are distressful; like a skilful sailor, who trims his sails to a wind he cannot change and thus forces it to carry him on his way, we use the circumstances we cannot alter by adapting ourselves to them in such fashion that they are compelled to help us.

Thus are we partly compelled and partly free. We must work amid and with the conditions which we have created, but we are free within them to work upon them. We ourselves, eternal Spirits, are inherently free, but we can only work in and through the thought-nature, the desire-nature, and the physical nature, which we have created; these are our materials and our tools, and we can have none other till we make these anew.

Out of the Past

Another point of great importance to remember is that the karma of the past is of very mixed character; we have not to breast a single current, the totality of the past, but a stream made up of currents running in various directions, some opposing us, some helping us; the effective force we have to face, the resultant left when all these oppositions have neutralized each other, may be one which it is by no means beyond our present power to overcome. Face to face with a piece of evil karma from the past, we should ever grapple with it, striving to overcome it, remembering that it embodies only a part of our past, and that other parts of that past are with us, strengthening and invigorating us for the contest. The present effort, added to those forces from the past, may be, often is, just enough to overcome the opposition.

Or, again, an opportunity presents itself, and we hesitate to take advantage of it, fearing that our resources are inadequate to discharge the responsibilities it brings; but it would not be there unless our karma had brought it to us, the fruit of a past desire; let us seize it bravely and tenaciously, and we shall find that the very effort has awakened latent powers slumbering within us, unknown to us and needing a stimulus from outside to arouse them into activity. So many of our powers, created by effort in the past, are on the verge of expression and only need opportunity to flower into action.

We should always aim at a little more than we think we can do—not at a thing wholly beyond our present powers, but at that which seems to be just out of reach. As we work to achieve it, all the karmic force acquired in the past comes to our aid to strengthen us. The fact that we can nearly do a thing means that we have worked for it in the past, and the accumulated strength of those past efforts is within us. That we can do a little means the power of doing more; and even if we fail, the power put forth to the utmost passes into the reservoir of our forces, and the failure of to-day means the victory of to-morrow.

When circumstances are adverse, the same thing holds good ; we may have reached the point where one more effort means success. Therefore did Bhishma counsel effort under all conditions, and utter the encouraging phrase : " Exertion is greater than destiny." The result of many past exertions is embodied in our karma, and the present exertion added to them may make our force adequate for the achievement of our aim.

There are cases where the force of the karma of the past is so strong that no effort of the present can suffice to overbear it. Yet should effort be made, since few know when one of these cases is upon them, and, at the worst, the effort made diminishes that karmic force for the future. A chemist often labours for years to discover a force, or an arrangement of matter, which will enable him to achieve a result at which he is aiming. He is often thwarted, but he does not acknowledge himself defeated. He cannot change the chemical elements ; he cannot change the laws of chemical combination ; he accepts these ungrudgingly, and there lies " the sublime patience of the investigator ". But the knowledge of the investigator, ever-increasing by virtue of his patient experiments, at last touches the point where it enables him to bring about the desired result. Precisely the same spirit should be acquired by the student of karma ;

he should accept the inevitable without complaint, but untiredly seek the methods whereby his aim may be secured, sure that his only limitation is his ignorance, and that perfect knowledge must mean perfect power.

Old Friendships

Another fact of the greatest importance is that we are brought by karma into touch with people whom we have known in the past, to some of whom we owe debts, some of whom owe debts to us. No man treads his long pilgrimage alone, and the egos to whom he is linked by many ties in a common past come from all parts of the world to surround him in the present. We have known someone in the past who has gone ahead of us in evolution; perchance we then did him some service, and a karmic tie was formed. In the present, that tie draws us within the orbit of his activity, and we receive from outside us a new impulse of force, a power, not our own, impelling us to listen and to obey.

Many of such helpful karmic links have we seen within the Theosophical Society. Long, long ago, He who is now the Master K. H. was taken prisoner in a battle with an Egyptian army, and was generously befriended and sheltered by an Egyptian of high rank. Thousands of years later, help is needed for the nascent Theosophical Society, and the Master, looking over India for one to aid in the great work, sees His old friend of the Egyptian and other lives, now Mr. A. P. Sinnett, editing the leading Anglo-Indian newspaper, *The Pioneer*. Mr. Sinnett goes, as usual, to Simla; Mme. Blavatsky goes up thither, to form the link; Mr. Sinnett is drawn within the immediate influence of the Master, receives instruction from Him, and becomes the author of *The Occult World* and of *Esoteric Buddhism*, carrying to thousands the message of Theosophy. Such rights we win by help given in the past, the right to help in higher ways and with further-reaching effects, while we ourselves are also helped by the tightening of ancient links of friendship won by service, royally recompensed by that priceless gift of knowledge, gained by one and shed abroad for many.

We Grow by Giving

In truth, in this world of law, where action and reaction are equal, all help which is given comes back to the giver, as a ball thrown against a wall bounds back to the hand of the thrower. That which we give returns to us; hence, even for a selfish reason, it is well to give, and to give abundantly. "Cast thy bread upon the waters, and thou shalt find it after many days." To give, even from a selfish motive, is good, for it leads to an interchange of worthy human feelings, by which both giver and receiver grow and expand, so that the Divine within each has opportunity of larger expression. Even though the gift at first be a matter of calculation—"He that hath pity upon the poor lendeth unto the Lord: and look, what he layeth out, it shall be paid him again"—yet gradually the love evoked shall make future giving spontaneous and unselfish, and thus karmic links of love shall bind ego to ego in the long series of human lives. All personal links, whether of love or hate, grow out of the past, and in each life we strengthen the ties that bind us to our friends and ensure our return together in the lives that lie in front. Thus do we build up a true family, outside all ties of blood, and return to earth over and over again to knit closer the ancient bonds.

Collective Karma

Before completing this imperfect study we must consider what is termed Collective Karma, the complex into which are woven the results of the collective thoughts, desires and activities of groups, whether large or small. The principles at work are the same, but the factors are far more numerous, and this multiplicity immensely increases the difficulty of understanding the effects.

The idea of considering a group as a larger individual is not alien from modern science, and such larger individuals generate karma along lines similar to those which we have been studying. A family, a nation, a sub-race, a race, are all but larger individuals, each having a past behind it, the creator of its present, each with a future ahead of it, now in course of creation. An ego coming into such a larger individual must share in its general karma ; his own special karma has brought him into it and must be worked out within it, the larger karma often offering conditions which enable the smaller to act.

FAMILY KARMA

Let us consider the collective karma of a family. The family has a thought-atmosphere of its own, into the colouring of which enter family traditions and customs, family ways of regarding the external world, family pride in the past, a strong sense of family honour. All the thought-forms of a member of the family will be influenced by these conditions, built up perhaps through hundreds of years, and shaping, moulding, colouring, all the thoughts, desires and activities of the individual newly born into it. Tendencies in him that conflict with family traditions will be suppressed, all unconsciously to him; the things "a fellow cannot do" will have for him no attraction; he will be lifted above various temptations, and the seeds of evil which such temptations might have vivified in him will quietly atrophy away. The collective karma of the family will provide him with opportunities for distinction, open out avenues of usefulness, bring him advantages in the struggle for life, and ensure his success. How has he come into conditions so favourable? It may be by a personal tie with some one already there, a service rendered in a previous life, a bond of affection, an unexhausted relationship. This avails to draw him into the circle, and he then profits by the various karmic results which belong to the family in virtue of its collective past, of the courage, ability, usefulness of some of its members, that have left an inheritance of social consideration as a family heirloom.

Where the family karma is bad the individual born into it suffers, as in the former case he profits, and the collective karma hinders, as in the former instance it promoted, his welfare.

In both cases the individual will usually have built up in himself characteristics which demand for their full exercise the environment provided by the family. But a very strong personal tie, or unusual service, might, without this, draw a man into a family wherein was his beneficiary, and so give him an opportunity which, generally, he had not deserved, but had won by this special act of his past.

National Karma

Let us think on the collective karma of a nation. Face to face with this, the individual is comparatively helpless, for nothing he can do can free him from this, and he must trim his sails to it as best he may. Even a Master can but slightly modify national karma, or change the national atmosphere.

The rise and fall of nations are brought about by collective karma. Acts of national righteousness or of national criminality, led up to by noble or base thinking, largely directed by national ideals, bring about national ascent or national descent. The actions of the Spanish Inquisition, the driving of the Jews and of the Moors out of Spain, the atrocious cruelties accompanying the conquests of Mexico and Peru—all these were national crimes which dragged Spain down from its splendid position of power and reduced it to comparative powerlessness.

Seismic changes—earthquakes, volcanoes, floods—or national catastrophes like famine and plague, all are cases of collective karma, brought about by great streams of thoughts and actions of a collective rather than an individual character.

As with a family, so with a nation to a much greater degree, will there be an atmosphere created by the nation's past; and national traditions, customs, view-points, will exercise a vast influence on the minds of all who dwell within the nation. Few individuals can free themselves wholly from these influences and consider a question affecting the nation without any bias, or see it from a standpoint other than that of their own people. Hence largely arise international quarrels and suspicions, mistaken views, and distorted opinions of the motives of another nation. Many a war has broken out in consequence of the differences in the thought-atmospheres surrounding the prospective combatants, and these difficulties are multiplied when the nations spring from different racial stocks, as, say, the Italians and the Turks. All the knower of karma can do in these cases is to realize the fact that his opinions and views are largely the product of the larger individuality of his nation and to check this bias as much as he can, giving full weight to the views obtained from the standpoint of the antagonistic nation.

When a man finds himself in the grip of a national karma which he cannot resist—say that he is a member of a conquered nation—he should calmly study the causes which have led to the national subjugation, and should set to work to remedy them, endeavouring to influence public opinion along lines which will eradicate these causes.

INDIA'S KARMA

There was an article published in *East and West*—Mr. Malabari's paper—some time ago on the national karma of India, which was an admirable example of the way in which national karma should *not* be regarded. It was said that the national karma of India was that it should be conquered—obviously true, else the conquest of India would not have taken place—and that it should therefore accept its lot of service, and not try to change any of the existing conditions—as obviously wrong. The knower of karma would say: The Indians were not the original possessors of this country; they came down from Central Asia, conquering the land, subduing its then peoples, and reducing them to servitude; during thousands of years they conquered and ruled, and they generated a national karma. They trod down the conquered tribes, and made them slaves, oppressing them and taking advantage of them. The bad karma thus made brought down upon them in turn many invaders. Greeks, Mughals, Portuguese, Dutch, French, English—they all came, and fought, and conquered, and possessed. Still the lesson of karma has not been learned, though the millions of the untouchables are a standing proof of the wrongs inflicted on them. Now the Indians ask for a share in the government of their own country, and they are hampered by this bad national karma. Let them, then, while asking for the growth of freedom for themselves, atone to these untouchables by giving them social freedom and lifting them in the social scale. A national effort must remove this national evil, and do away with a continuing cause of national weakness. India must redeem the wrong she has done, and cleanse her hands from oppression; so shall she change her national karma, and build the foundation of freedom. Karma will work for freedom and not against it, when the karma generated by oppression is changed into the karma made by uplifting and respecting. Public feeling can be changed, and every man who speaks graciously and kindly to an inferior is helping to change it. Meanwhile all whose own individual karma has brought them into the nation should recognize facts as they are, but should set to work to change those that are undesirable. National karma may be changed, like individual karma, but as the causes are of longer continuance, so must be the effects, and the new causes introduced can only slowly modify the results outgrowing from the past.

National Disasters

The karma which brings about seismic catastrophes and other national disasters includes in its sweep vast numbers of individuals whose special karma contains sudden death, disease, or prolonged physical suffering. It is interesting and instructive to notice the way in which people who have not such karmic liabilities are called away from the scene of a great catastrophe, while others are hurried into it; when an earthquake slays a number of people there will be cases of "miraculous escape"—one called away by a telegram, by urgent business, etc.—and of equally miraculous tossing of victims into the place in time for their slaying. If such calling away proved to be impossible, then some special arrangement at the moment guarded from death—a beam keeping off falling stones, or the like.

When a natural catastrophe is impending, people with appropriate individual karma are gathered together in the place, as in the flood at Johnstown, Pa., or the great earthquake and fire at San Francisco. In an earthquake in the north of India a few years ago, there were some victims who had posted back in hot haste—to be killed. Others left the place the night before—to be saved from death. The local catastrophe is used to work off particular karmas. Or a carriage taking a man to the station is stopped in a street block, and he misses the train. He is angry, but the train is wrecked and he is saved. It is not that the block was there in order to stop him, but that the block was utilized for the purpose. At Messina some who were not to die were dug out days afterwards, and in more than one case food had come to maintain life, brought by an astral agent. In shipwrecks, again, safety or death will depend on individual karma. Sometimes an ego has a debt of sudden death to pay, but it has not been included in the debts to be discharged during the present incarnation; his presence in some accident brought about by a collective karma offers the opportunity of discharging the debt "out of due time". The ego prefers to seize the opportunity and to get rid of the karma, and his body is struck away with the rest.

How the Ego Selects

Individual characteristics developed in one life may bring their owner in another life into a nation which offers peculiar facilities for their exercise. Thus a man who had developed a strong concrete mind, apt for commerce, say, in the vaishya (merchant) caste in India, may be thrown down into the United States of America, and there become a Rockefeller. In his new personality he will see that vast wealth is only tolerable when used for national purposes, and he will carry out in America the vaishya ideal that the man who has gathered huge wealth becomes a steward in the national household, to distribute wisely for the general benefit the stores accumulated as personal possessions. Thus the old ideal will be planted in the midst of a new civilization, and will spread abroad through another people.

ENGLAND'S KARMA

A colonizing nation, like England, will often be guilty of much cruelty in the seizing of lands belonging to the savage tribes that the colonists drive out. Thousands perish prematurely during the conquest and subsequent settlement. These have a karmic claim against England collectively, as well as the debts due from the actual assailants. They are drawn to England and take birth in her slums, providing a population of congenital criminals, of non-moral and feeble-minded people.

The debt due to them by the summary closing of their previous existences should be paid by education and training, thus quickening their evolution and lifting them out of their natural savagery.

The French Revolution

The collective selfishness and indifference of the well-to-do towards the poor and miserable, leaving them to fester in overcrowded slums, among degrading and evil-provoking surroundings, bring down upon themselves social troubles, labour unrest, threatening combinations. Carried to excess in France during the reigns of Louis XIV and Louis XV, this same selfishness and indifference were the direct causes of the French Revolution, of the destruction of the Crown and of the nobility.

Taught by Theosophy to see the workings of karmic law in the history of nations as well as in that of individuals, we should be forces making for national welfare and prosperity. The strongest karmic cause is the power of thought, and this is as true for nations as for individuals. To hold up

A Noble National Ideal

is to set going the most powerful karmic force, for into such an ideal the thoughts of many are ever flowing, and it becomes stronger by the daily influx. Public opinion continually changes under the flow of its influences, and reproduces that which is constantly held up for its admiration. The thought-force accumulates until it becomes irresistible, and lifts the whole nation upwards to a higher level.

The knowers of karma can work deliberately and consciously, sure of their ground, sure of their methods, relying on the Good Law. Thus they become conscious co-operators with the Divine Will which works in evolution, and are filled with a deep peace and an unending joy.

Printed by D. V. Syamala Rau, at the Vasanta Press,
The Theosophical Society, Adyar, Madras.